VIDEO COMPANION B

W9-BHZ-540

NCCL
Echoes of Faith™

PRAYER AND SPIRITUALITY

Sr. Edith Prendergast, R.S.C.

Content Specialist
Bishop Robert F. Morneau

Contributor
Rev. Robert J. Hater, Ph.D.

Project Director
Jo McClure Rotunno

Project Editor
Judy Deckers

NATIONAL CONFERENCE OF CATECHETICAL LEADERSHIP

RESOURCES FOR CHRISTIAN LIVING™

Allen, Texas

NIHIL OBSTAT
Rev. Msgr. Glenn D. Gardner, J.C.D.
Censor Librorum

IMPRIMATUR
† Most Rev. Charles V. Grahmann
Bishop of Dallas

March 16, 1998

The Nihil Obstat and Imprimatur are official declarations that the material reviewed is free
of doctrinal or moral error. No implication is contained therein that those granting the Nihil
Obstat and Imprimatur agree with the contents, opinions, or statements expressed.

Design: Dennis Davidson

ACKNOWLEDGMENTS

Scripture quotations are from the New Revised Standard Version of the Bible, copyright
© 1989 by the division of Christian Education of the National Council of the Churches of
Christ in the USA. Used by permission; all rights reserved.

Excerpts from the English translation of the *Catechism of the Catholic Church* for the United
States of America, copyright © 1994 United States Catholic Conference, Inc.—Libreria
Editrice Vaticana. Used with permission.

Excerpts from the *Documents of Vatican II,* Walter M. Abbott, S.J. General Editor, copyright
© 1966 Herder and Herder. All rights reserved.

The Angelus is from *Catholic Household Blessings & Prayers,* Washington D.C.: USCC, 1988,
excerpted from the English translation of *A Book of Prayers* © 1982, International Committee
on English in the Liturgy, Inc. (ICEL).

The story contained in the article by Rev. Robert J. Hater, "A Thankful Heart," in this
booklet originally appeared in his book *The Search for Meaning: Myth and Mystery in the New
Millennium,* published by Crossroad Publishing, 370 Lexington Avenue, New York, NY,
10017–6503, copyright 1998. Used with permission.

Send all inquiries to:
RCL • Resources for Christian Living ™
200 East Bethany Drive
Allen, Texas 75002-3804

Toll Free   800-822-6701
Fax   800-688-8356

Printed in the United States of America

#10095	ISBN 0-7829-0613-3	*I Believe/We Believe* Video
#301	ISBN 0-7829-0616-8	*I Believe/We Believe* Booklet
#10096	ISBN 0-7829-0859-4	*Liturgy and Sacraments* Video
#302	ISBN 0-7829-0858-6	*Liturgy and Sacraments* Booklet
#10097	ISBN 0-7829-0862-4	*Catholic Morality* Video
#303	ISBN 0-7829-0861-6	*Catholic Morality* Booklet
#10098	ISBN 0-7829-0865-9	*Prayer and Spirituality* Video
#304	ISBN 0-7829-0864-0	*Prayer and Spirituality* Booklet
#10099	ISBN 0-7829-0868-3	*Introduction to the Scriptures* Video
#305	ISBN 0-7829-0867-5	*Introduction to the Scriptures* Booklet

1 2 3 4 5   02 01 00 99 98

CONTENTS

Letter iv

Preface v

Overview vi

Opening Prayer vii

Before You Begin viii

1. What Is Prayer?
Introduction 1
Looking Ahead 2
Looking Back 4
"The Heart of Prayer" by Jo McClure Rotunno ... 6
Looking Beyond 8

2. How Do We Pray?
Introduction 9
Looking Ahead 10
Looking Back 12
"Contemplation: Looking at God with Love"
    by Sr. Edith Prendergast, R.S.C. 14
Looking Beyond 16

3. The Prayerful Life
Introduction 17
Looking Ahead 18
Looking Back 20
"A Thankful Heart" by Rev. Robert J. Hater 22
Looking Beyond 24

4. The Our Father
Introduction 25
Looking Ahead 26
Looking Back 28
"Reflections on the Our Father"
    by Bishop Robert F. Morneau 30
Looking Beyond 34

Closing Reflection 35

Resource Bibliography 38

Assessment Tool 39

NCCL

Dear Catechist,

In his letter on catechesis, our Holy Father, John Paul II, said, "As the twentieth century draws to a close, the Church is bidden by God and by events . . . to offer catechesis her best resources in people and energy, without sparing effort, toil or material means, in order to organize it better and to train qualified personnel" (*On Catechesis in Our Time*, 15). The National Conference of Catechetical Leadership (NCCL) believes that you, the catechist, are the most important resource.

As one entrusted with the responsibility and honor of proclaiming the message of Jesus and his Church, we know you want to do your very best to prepare yourself to be an effective catechist. *Echoes of Faith* provides you with an opportunity to increase your knowledge of the Catholic faith and your skills for sharing that faith with adults, youth, or children.

We have designed this program for use in varied settings. If you are working alone on a module, it is important that you link up with someone (your local DRE, catechist trainer, parish priest, etc.) so that you do not make the journey alone.

Be assured that the worldwide community of catechists supports you in prayer and memory. We depend on you to bring "tidings of great joy" in the classrooms, religious education centers, homes, and wherever catechesis takes place.

Thomas P. Walters
Thomas P. Walters
NCCL President

Edmund F. Gordon
Edmund F. Gordon
NCCL Project Director

A project of the National Conference of Catechetical Leadership

Produced by RCL • Resources for Christian Living™

PREFACE

Echoes of Faith is a basic-level, video-assisted resource for the formation and enrichment of catechists in parishes and Catholic schools. It can also provide a vehicle for adult faith formation. It is being developed and sponsored by the National Conference of Catechetical Leadership (NCCL) and produced by RCL • Resources for Christian Living. The goal of the theological modules is to acquaint adults with the foundations of Catholic doctrine and Tradition. *Echoes of Faith* combines videos with companion booklets. The booklet prepares you for viewing the video, invites you to record your responses to the video, provides pertinent articles to enrich your understanding, and helps you apply the material to life and to your catechetical settings. Each theology module should take at least four hours to complete. The following is the format for each of the four segments in the booklet.

INTRODUCTION

Before watching each segment of the video, read the introduction to each segment. It will introduce you to the topic to be explored, help you to identify what you already know about the topic, and focus on what you can hope to gain from that segment.

LOOKING AHEAD

As immediate preparation for viewing the video segment, the video outline alerts you to some key concepts that are going to be presented. You are also invited to record on these pages your initial thoughts and reflections on the content of the video segment.

LOOKING BACK

This section invites you to record your reflections and clarify your thoughts about the material presented. Respond to one or more of these questions before moving on to the next portion of the video.

ENRICHMENT ARTICLE

A short article reinforces and expands the content presented in the video segment.

LOOKING BEYOND

This page invites you to begin to apply your ideas about what you have learned.

Bishop Robert F. Morneau was ordained auxiliary bishop of Green Bay, Wisconsin, on February 22, 1979. He has served as diocesan director for religious in Green Bay and as an instructor of philosophy at Silver Lake College in Manitowoc, Wisconsin. He has also taught at the Summer Theological Institute of St. Norbert's Abbey in De Pere, Wisconsin. Bishop Morneau's writings appear frequently in such periodicals as Contemplative Review, Review for Religious, Sisters Today, Spiritual Life, *and* Pastoral Life Magazine. *He is very popular as a retreat director and lecturer throughout the United States.*

OVERVIEW

This module explores the relationship with the living God, which we call prayer. It is placed within the context of one's spirituality, the name we give to the entire life lived in response to God's call. Prayer and spirituality are our wholehearted "yes" to the mystery of God seeking us. We express this mystery in our creeds, celebrate it in our liturgy, and live it out as we attempt to follow the way of Jesus Christ to the Father, in the Spirit.

This module is divided into four segments. The first two explore the nature of prayer, various forms of prayer, and some obstacles to prayer. The third segment examines the spiritual life as it is lived in the midst of day-to-day issues and challenges. The final segment offers a reflection and catechesis on the central prayer of the Christian tradition, the Our Father.

The module will address the following topics:

- ❖ The basic dynamic of prayer is listening and responding to God's call.
- ❖ The Angelus prayer of our tradition demonstrates the dynamic of prayer.
- ❖ Mary is the perfect model of acceptance and response to God's call.
- ❖ Personal prayer is always joined to the community of faith.

- ❖ There are various prayer forms through which we make our response to God.
- ❖ Our life experience places obstacles in the way of our prayer.
- ❖ The Holy Spirit is the source of our prayer response.
- ❖ The three foundations of the spiritual life are prayer, service, and asceticism.
- ❖ The Our Father is the bedrock of Christian prayer.

This presentation is only an introduction to these themes. However, through the process of reflection on this content provided by this booklet, you should better understand these principles and feel more confident in sharing them with others.

The *Catechism of the Catholic Church,* Part Four: Christian Prayer, further reading, as well as reflection, and attendance in classes and workshops will help you to deepen your understanding. This continued reflection will further increase your confidence in applying this knowledge in your own prayerful response to God's call.

Although you may be alone as you watch this video or use this booklet, you are advised to meet regularly with a companion or member of your faith community to share your insights about your Catholic faith.

Name of Program Director, School Principal, or Companion:

_____

Telephone:

_____

Opening Prayer

The Magnificat
Mary's Song of Praise

My soul magnifies the Lord,
and my spirit rejoices in God my Savior,
for he has looked with favor
on the lowliness of his servant.
Surely, from now on all generations
will call me blessed;
for the Mighty One has done
great things for me,
and holy is his name.
His mercy is for those who fear him
from generation to generation.
He has shown strength with his arm;
he has scattered the proud
in the thoughts of their hearts.
He has brought down the powerful
from their thrones,
and lifted up the lowly;
he has filled the hungry with good things,
and sent the rich away empty.
He has helped his servant Israel,
in remembrance of his mercy,
according to the promise he made
to our ancestors,
to Abraham and to his descendants forever.

LUKE 1:46–55

Edith Prendergast, a Religious Sister of Charity, is Director of the Office of Religious Education for the Archdiocese of Los Angeles. A native of Ireland, Sr. Edith has been involved in religious education and spiritual formation in the United States for over thirty years. She holds a master's degree in Theology from Boston College, and a Certificate in Spiritual Formation from St. Louis University, St. Louis, Missouri. She has also worked as a parish director of religious education, a high school teacher, and a youth minister. She served as a collaborator on The Challenge of Adolescent Catechesis: Maturing in Faith, developed by the National Federation for Catholic Youth Ministry. In recent years, Sr. Edith has been involved in retreat work and spiritual direction, and offers workshops nationally in the areas of spirituality and spiritual formation.

BEFORE YOU BEGIN

Underneath each of the ages listed below, write a sentence or two describing prayer as you experienced it at that time in your life.

❖ Seven years old

❖ Thirteen years old

❖ Twenty-one years old

❖ Today

WHAT IS PRAYER?

Prayer is listening and responding to God. It is listening with an openness to hear God's Word calling to us. Sometimes God seems to speak loudly and clearly through the words of Scripture or the events of our lives. At other times God's Word comes to us in a gentle breeze or a still silent voice, as the prophet Elijah experienced (1 Kings 19:9–13).

We are called to listen at all times for the voice of God. This listening involves an openness of heart, a risking to be ourselves, a yielding, and a willingness to be changed. We come to prayer just as we are, with our hopes, fears, joys, and doubts. God speaks, and invites us to respond with a "yes" to God's offer of love. Our response involves a willingness to spend time with God, pondering the words of Scripture, discerning God's message to us, and opening up our lives to God's transforming power.

In the Catholic Tradition, Mary is our model of prayer. The ancient prayer of the Angelus recalls Mary's response to the angel Gabriel. Traditionally prayed at intervals during the day, it reminds us of Mary's intimacy with God and the response each of us is called to make to God's offer of love.

LEARNING OBJECTIVES
After completing the first segment of this module, you will be able to:

1. Appreciate more deeply God's presence in all of creation

2. Define prayer as listening and responding to God's call

3. Explain why Mary is our model of prayer

4. Describe the importance of praying throughout the day

YOUR THOUGHTS
Spend a few moments thinking about the following.

Think of a time when you listened to God in prayer, and when you felt that God listened to you. Describe your experience.

🖎

The life of prayer is the habit of being in the presence of the thrice-holy God and in communion with him.

CATECHISM OF THE CATHOLIC CHURCH (CCC) 2565

LOOKING AHEAD

This video segment suggests a response to the general question, "What is prayer?" You will find an outline of this video content below. You may wish to refer to this outline as you view the video. Use the space provided to jot down any questions or thoughts that occur to you during your viewing. When you have finished, record your initial reactions to the video before moving on to the questions on pages 4 and 5.

VIDEO OUTLINE

God's Call and Our Response

God speaks to us through all of God's creation.

We can only respond to God because God first speaks to us.

Prayer is listening and responding to God's call heard deep within us.

Mary and the Angelus

The Angelus, a prayer form dating from the thirteenth century, recalls the moment when Mary accepted God's call to be the mother of the Savior.

The Angelus prayer is said at the beginning, middle, and end of the day.

The Angelus is a way of marking time with a reminder of God's invitation to all of us to respond in faith.

The Angelus reminds us that Mary is our model of prayer.

Our Prayer

All prayer, like Mary's, is a profound act of faith.

Like Mary, our "yes" to God is a lifelong commitment of our whole selves to God.

Jesus offered his Mother to the community of faith at the end of his life.

Even our personal prayer is never completely private prayer, for we are connected at all times to the believing community by our Baptism.

THOUGHTS AND QUESTIONS DURING VIEWING

Glory of God found in Humans fully alive

Listens & Responds

We say yes & life changes - pray

committment to

Pray arises out of faith & love of God

Committment of self

Daily life calls & we respond

Respond to God fully committed to God

FIRST IMPRESSIONS AFTER VIEWING

Prayer listening & responding to Gods call

in everyday

God calls we respond

Pause - Beging - Middle & end

Listen

Respond to voice of God

Not an escape from life

LOOKING BACK

Then Mary said,
"Here am I,
the servant of the Lord;
let it be with me
according to your word."

LUKE 1:38

Review the questions or comments that occurred to you as you viewed this video segment. When time allows, discuss your thoughts with another person. Now respond to several of the questions or activities below. Return to the remaining items throughout the year as a way of deepening your understanding.

1. God speaks to us in all of creation. How do you create opportunities in your daily life to hear the voice of God speaking to you?

Get up Early to meditate on day's readings

2. Like Mary, our prayer must begin, "Let it be . . ." What situation in your own life is calling you to speak those words right now?

Let it be according to God's will
at work not my will or
Boss's will

3. The Church teaches us that our personal prayer is always joined with the prayer of the community. Describe some times in your life when you have been strengthened by that knowledge.

Prayer of faithful

Prayer Chain

4. God speaks within us and all around us. From the following list, choose one occasion when you have heard God speaking to you. Write a prayer of thanksgiving for the word that God spoke to you at that time.

❖ A time of inner struggle

❖ A walk amid the beauty of nature — *Thank you for the stars, moon, animals flowers & all your nature*

❖ A moment of great joy

*For it was you who
formed
my inward parts;
you knit me together
in my mother's womb.
I praise you,
for I am fearfully and
wonderfully made.*

PSALM 139:13–14

The article on the next page will increase your understanding of the nature of prayer.

▶ ▶ ▶ ▶ ▶ ▶ ▶

THE HEART OF PRAYER

by Jo McClure Rotunno

Saint John Damascene called prayer "a raising of the mind and heart to God." Saint Therese of Lisieux called it "a surge of the heart." The *Catechism of the Catholic Church* affirms that the wellspring of prayer lies in the human heart, that seat of the soul or "hidden center" where only the Spirit of God can go. (*CCC*, 2563)

Sacred Scripture shows us that the origins of human prayer arise in history after the entry of sin into the world. From this moment, God desires to restore us to friendship. In the Hebrew Scriptures we learn the qualities of a prayerful life. From Abel we learn that prayer is walking with God. From Abraham and Sarah we discover attentiveness of heart and conformity to God's will. From Jacob we learn that prayer can be a "wrestling" with God, but that perseverance has its rewards. In Moses we find a deep intimacy with God and see the power of intercession as Moses brings the needs of the people before God. From Samuel we learn the importance of listening for God, whose Word often comes as a whisper rather than an earthquake. From David we learn both

how to praise and how to repent. From the prophets we learn of righteousness, and the power to proclaim the truth that is born of intimacy with God.

In the Psalms we find an entire school of prayer, so much so that some have said that all study of the Scriptures should begin with the Psalms. These masterpieces of prayer both nourish and speak the prayer of a community of faith. While they arose in a particular time and place, they have become universal expressions of praise and thanksgiving, of lamentation and repentance. In the Psalms, the Word of God becomes our word—our prayer (*CCC*, 2587).

Jesus is the perfect model of prayer. Jesus, though Son of God, was human like us. He took his first steps in prayer as we do, learning from his family and his religious tradition. Jesus found God in his human heart, where he discovered his deep intimacy, with his Father. He shows us the way to that intimacy, which is available to all of us who are willing to make the journey.

When did Jesus pray? He prayed before all the decisive moments in his ministry, most

Jo McClure Rotunno is Director of Electronic Media Products for RCL • Resources for Christian Living™. She serves as project director for the Echoes of Faith *program. She has been a religious educator for thirty years. Jo worked as a religious education consultant for the Office of Religious Education in Los Angeles, and served there for twenty years in the formation of catechists and master catechists. She speaks nationally on topics related to catechist formation and enrichment. Jo holds an M.A. in Religious Studies from Mount St. Mary's College in Los Angeles.*

memorably before his Passion. He prayed before the great moments in the ministry of his disciples. He spent an entire night alone in prayer before the call of the Twelve. The night he was betrayed he told Peter he had prayed that Peter's faith would be strong, that this man to whom he must entrust so much would not be tempted.

Where and how did Jesus pray? Jesus often prayed in solitude, sometimes apart from others, often at night. All of his words and works were empowered by these times of silent prayer. One of the great public prayers of Jesus occurs at the raising of Lazarus (John 11:41–42). Here Jesus teaches us that all prayer begins in thanksgiving. He acknowledges that in all cases "the Giver is more precious than the gift" (*CCC*, 2604); see Matthew 16:21, 33. And in all decisive situations, Jesus submits his own will to his Father's will.

Jesus taught his disciples how to pray. He reminded them of the constant conversion of heart that bringing the reign of God would require. He encouraged them to strive for great things in their prayer—to be bold. In the Lord's Prayer, he summarized for them his entire message, so much so that his disciples incorporated it into their worship from the very beginning. He cautioned them to be watchful in prayer, to be patient and humble as he had been. And he told them to always pray in his name, in the power of the Spirit which remains with us.

At the end of his earthly life, it was Jesus' prayer, spoken from the depths of his heart, that was heard by God and effected salvation for us all. He stayed faithful to the attitude of prayer he learned first from his mother: "Let it be with me according to your word" (Luke 1:38).

[O]ne rides the psalms like a river current, noticing in passing how alien these ancient and sophisticated texts are, and how utterly accessible.

KATHLEEN NORRIS

FOR REFLECTION

What insights have you gained from this article about the importance of prayer in the Christian life?

Turn the page to complete this segment of the module.

▶ ▶ ▶ ▶ ▶ ▶ ▶

LOOKING BEYOND

LOOKING BEYOND

If we are to become prayerful people, our hearts and minds must come together each day in silence and solitude.

ROBERT WICKS

LISTENING AND RESPONDING

During the next week, find a time to spend ten minutes alone in silent, prayerful thanksgiving. Afterward, describe your experience in this space.

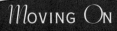

PRAYING WITH OTHERS

If you wished to encourage others to have a prayer experience similar to the one described above, list three suggestions you could give them to help them quiet themselves for this encounter with God.

❖

❖

❖

MOVING ON

THE FIRST SEGMENT SUGGESTED ANSWERS TO THE QUESTION, "WHAT IS PRAYER?" THE SECOND SEGMENT WILL INTRODUCE YOU TO SOME OF THE WAYS WE PRAY AND EXPLORE OBSTACLES TO PRAYER.

How Do We Pray?

Prayer arises from the center of our being and gives expression to all our human experiences. We praise and give thanks, knowing that all is gift from God. We give thanks in good times and in bad, because in faith we know that God is with us on our journey. Because God has blessed us, we also bless the One who is the giver of all good things.

Prayer is not always easy. Distractions, discouragement, and even laziness can stand in our way. But God is patient, and is present to us even when we fail to listen. We know we stand in need. This awareness of our poverty is gift as well, for it acknowledges our dependence on God as we ask for healing and forgiveness for ourselves and for others.

At the heart of prayer is the Eucharist, where we join the community in listening and responding to God's Word. We ask forgiveness for our sins. We listen to God's Word in the Scriptures. We bless and give thanks; we praise God's glory. We ask the Spirit to intercede for us. We offer all that we are and all that we do to God, joined with the Paschal mystery of God's own Son. The Eucharist nourishes us and challenges us to make our entire lives a prayer of blessing.

LEARNING OBJECTIVES
After completing this segment of the module, you will be able to:

1. Identify some of the traditional kinds of prayer

2. Examine some distractions to prayer

3. Appreciate the Eucharist as the prayer of the community

YOUR THOUGHTS
Spend a few moments thinking about the following.

Think of a time when you felt God did not respond to your needs. How did you feel? What did you learn about yourself and about God through that experience?

Blessed be the God and Father of our Lord Jesus Christ, who has blessed us in Christ with every spiritual blessing in the heavenly places.

EPHESIANS 1:3

LOOKING AHEAD

This video segment explores various kinds of prayer and common obstacles to prayer. You will find an outline of this video content below. You may wish to refer to this outline as you view the video. Use the space provided to jot down any questions or thoughts that occur to you during your viewing. When you have finished, record your initial reactions to the video before moving on to the questions on pages 12 and 13.

FORMS OF CHRISTIAN PRAYER

- ❖ BLESSING AND ADORATION.
- ❖ PRAISE
- ❖ THANKSGIVING
- ❖ PETITION
- ❖ INTERCESSION

VIDEO OUTLINE

Ways of Prayer

We see glimpses of God's grace within, around, and among us.

The principal forms of prayer in the Christian tradition are blessing or adoration, praise, thanksgiving, petition, and intercession.

God always speaks first in our prayer.

The three principal expressions of prayer are vocal prayer, meditation, and contemplation.

Growing in the Spiritual Life

The spiritual life requires work, effort, and attention.

Prayer is a serious dialogue with God leading to intimacy, which brings transformation.

Prayer requires discipline, but prayer also increases our perseverance.

Some obstacles to prayer are forgetfulness, frustration, discouragement, lack of concentration, laziness, dryness, and faulty expectations.

Two great helps in the life of prayer are the reading of Sacred Scripture and the willingness to give time to our relationship with God.

God is always faithful; God's love and grace are always being offered through the power of the Holy Spirit.

THOUGHTS AND QUESTIONS DURING VIEWING

[handwritten notes:]

Respond to movement of

Pray best from our lives

underneath our pray is God

Blessing
Praise
Thanksgiving
Petition — Pray of Sorrow
Intercession — ask for forgiveness

Service to community work — Prayer

obstacles to prayer —
Relationship with God takes work

FIRST IMPRESSIONS AFTER VIEWING

[handwritten notes:]

Prayer — need sacrifice
Prayer leads us through growth
God reaches out we respond
obstacle to pray
  work Effort + attention
Prayer — Spiritual living
Give time to prayer sacrifice + determination

anxiety gone peaceful three

❖ **SILENCE**
  TO BE ATTENTIVE AND LISTEN TO GOD
❖ **SOLITUDE**
  TO BE ALONE WITH GOD
❖ **SURRENDER**
  TO SAY YES TO GOD

Through prayer we become aware of the life of God within us and it is this God within us who allows us to recognize the God among us.

HENRI J. M. NOUWEN

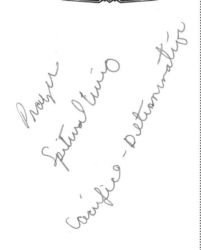

Review the questions or comments that occurred to you as you viewed this video segment. When time allows, discuss your thoughts with another person. Now respond to several of the questions or activities below. Return to the remaining items throughout the year as a way of deepening your understanding.

1. Reflecting on your own life of prayer, recall a time when you prayed each of the following kinds of prayer.
   ❖ Blessing — *family*
   ❖ Praise and thanksgiving — *Each thought for the day*
   ❖ Petition
   ❖ Intercession

2. Imagine a typical day in your life. What is going on in your life at each of the following times? Name those activities on the diagram below, and describe what your prayer at those times of day might be.

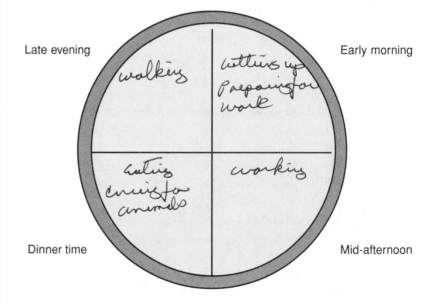

3. Name three obstacles you have encountered in your prayer life. What can you do to overcome these obstacles?

mind wondering off
Feel Repetitious

OBSTACLES TO PRAYER

❖ FORGETFULNESS
❖ DISTRACTIONS
❖ DISCOURAGEMENT
❖ LAZINESS
❖ DRYNESS
❖ FALSE EXPECTATIONS

4. On the video, Sr. Rosa Maria distinguished between knowing God and knowing *about* God. How do you understand the difference in these two ways of knowing God?

5. Many people create a space for prayer. Describe in your words or images the objects, music, and arrangement of space that would enhance your prayer.

Can—

The article on the next page will introduce you to contemplative prayer.

▶ ▶ ▶ ▶ ▶ ▶ ▶

CONTEMPLATION: LOOKING AT GOD WITH LOVE

by Edith Prendergast, R.S.C.

Contemplative prayer in my opinion is nothing else than a close sharing between friends; it means taking time frequently to be alone with him who we know loves us.

SAINT THERESE OF LISIEUX

Jesus' teaching on prayer in Luke's Gospel begins in the story of Jesus' visit to the two sisters, Martha and Mary. When Martha complains that Mary is not doing her share of serving, Jesus responds that Mary "has chosen the better part" (Luke 10:38–42). Mary is sitting at Jesus' feet, gazing at him and listening with love. That is contemplation.

In contemplation, the initiative always begins with God, who seeks to be an "insider" in our lives. Through contemplation we are brought into the heart of God, who speaks and invites us to respond. Christian contemplation is an interpersonal relationship with God, present to us here and now in Jesus Christ.

Saint Ignatius of Loyola, in his *Spiritual Exercises*, gives us a way to look at Jesus in the various "mysteries," or events of his life. He invites us to read a Scripture passage; imagine the scene; to use our senses to see, hear, taste, smell, and touch the experience being recounted; and to place ourselves in the scene and open our hearts to respond in love, awe, wonder, and gratitude.

Centering prayer is another way of entering into the mystery of God. Repeating a mantra such as the name of Jesus or a phrase such as "Be still and know that I am God" allows us to center on the person whose name we say, in whom our heart finds rest and solace. Contemplation calls us to "waste time" with God. Its form can be as simple as reciting the words of a psalm slowly, or taking a mindfulness walk where we tune in to the rhythm of our breathing and become aware of God's presence with us.

In contemplation we discover our utter dependence on God.

Solitude and silence are central to the development of a contemplative stance. The desert fathers and mothers moved away from the busyness of the city to commune with God in the starkness and emptiness of the desert. Most of us are not called to this radical lifestyle, but we are called to be contemplatives in action, which means to find God in all situations, relationships, and experiences of life. To do so, we must intentionally choose to build quiet times into our day. Our cars can become hermitages or places of refuge as we travel along the highway. Even our kitchens or offices can become places of contemplation for a few minutes during the day. A person on the street, the sight of a baby, a loving glance—all can provide moments of contemplation.

In contemplation, we discover our utter dependence on God. Julian of Norwich, the fourteenth century mystic, was overwhelmed by God's love for us. In one of her revelations she saw a hazelnut lying in her hand and realized that it was God's faithful love that prevented it, and indeed, everything else, from falling into nothingness.

In contemplative prayer, not only is God revealed to us, but we are revealed to ourselves. Knowing God's wondrous love for us makes us aware of our goodness, but also of our need for change and renewal. Such love demands receptivity, openness, and a belief that God is with us on the journey, both challenging and comforting us. We believe that as we stand before our God, we are transformed into God's likeness. From this place of transformation, we go forth to be bearers of good tidings, to image God to others, and to empower them to find God everywhere in life.

Contemplation is a "gaze" of faith, fixed on Jesus.

CCC, 2715

FOR REFLECTION

What is one practical thing you could do to make more room in your life for a more contemplative style of prayer?

Turn the page to complete this segment of the module.

*Vocal prayer
is an essential element
of the Christian life.*

CCC, 2701

LISTENING AND RESPONDING

Vocal prayer puts words in our innermost thoughts and feelings as we seek to engage in intimate conversation with God. What are some names with which you greet God in prayer when you are

❖ filled with joy?

❖ troubled and confused?

❖ in need of forgiveness?

PRAYING WITH OTHERS

Take each of the names of God that you created above and add words of petition or praise to it. Join your prayer to that of others in your group to create a litany you can pray together.

MOVING ON

THIS SEGMENT EXPLORED SOME WAYS WE PRAY AND SOME OBSTACLES TO PRAYER. THE NEXT SEGMENT WILL EXPLORE WAYS OF INTEGRATING AN ATTITUDE OF PRAYER-FULNESS INTO THE ACTIVITY OF DAILY LIFE.

THE PRAYERFUL LIFE

For the Christian, the spiritual life is the response of the whole person to God—body and soul. It involves our thoughts, our feelings, and our actions. Jesus was not a disembodied spirit; he was the *incarnate* God. His entire life and being was a response to God's love, and so must our lives be.

Christian spirituality could be compared to the three legs of a milking stool. It is first and foremost a relationship with God, nurtured by prayer. Second, it is a relationship with others, characterized by a life of service and ministry. Third, it is a relationship within ourselves, characterized by an asceticism or discipline that leads to life and freedom. These three—prayer, service, and asceticism—lay the foundations for the spiritual life.

Prayer reveals God to us, and also reveals us to ourselves. In prayer we discover the places in our lives in need of conversion and healing. We are sometimes like cluttered houses with no room for God, held captive by people, things, and our need to accumulate. Through asceticism, we learn what we must let go of, what discipline we must practice in order to respond to God's voice. From this stance we can go forth to be a word of God, to do the truth in love, to put on the mind of Jesus and to live for one another.

LEARNING OBJECTIVES
After completing this segment of the module, you will be able to:

1. Describe prayer, service, and asceticism as the three aspects of the spiritual life

2. Identify ways in which the spiritual life is both a personal and communal response to God's love

3. Understand more clearly the path of your own spiritual life

YOUR THOUGHTS
Spend a few moments thinking about the following.

What practices do you have that are related to your prayer life?

Abba Elias said, "What can sin do where there is penitence? And of what use is love where there is pride?"

THE SAYINGS OF THE DESERT FATHERS

LOOKING AHEAD

Even when it is lived out "in secret" (MATTHEW 6:6), prayer is always the prayer "of the Church;" it is a communion with the Holy Trinity.

CCC, 2655

(SEE GENERAL INTRODUCTION TO THE "LITURGY OF THE HOURS," 9).

Prayer can Transform crisis →

Families know

Prayer in politics serving common good Raising moral

expands cultures

Daily habits of prayer deepen

This segment explores the foundations of the spiritual life. You will find an outline of this video content below. You may wish to refer to this outline as you view the video. Use the space provided to jot down any questions or thoughts that occur to you during your viewing. When you have finished, record your initial reactions to the video before moving on to the questions on pages 20 and 21.

VIDEO OUTLINE

Introduction

No prayer is completely private. In all cases we are connected to one another in prayer through our baptism.

Prayer flows from our lives as believers.

The three key aspects of a healthy Christian spirituality are prayer, service, and asceticism.

Governor John Gilligan's Reflections on the Spiritual Life

We learn from childhood on that our relationship with God is not private; we are part of a community.

The ability to pray in times of great crisis is a gift.

Christian parents are called to nurture the life of God that lies in the hearts of their children.

We all owe a debt to the community that we should repay in every way we can.

All politics raises moral questions and attempts to resolve them for the common good.

All the world's peoples have religious and cultural gifts to offer.

Prayer and religious discipline help maintain and deepen our relationship with God.

THOUGHTS AND QUESTIONS DURING VIEWING

No prayer private

one part faith is nurtured

Prayer denied asceticism

Prayer can transform crisis situation

Families

*Christian & Catholic faith hard to
live in but good to die in*

infinite value - unique

FIRST IMPRESSIONS AFTER VIEWING

Spiritual discipline

LOOKING BACK

> *H*e "prays without ceasing" who unites prayer to works and good works to prayer.
>
> ORIGEN

Review the questions or comments that occurred to you as you viewed this video segment. When time allows, discuss your thoughts with another person. Now respond to several of the questions or activities below. Return to the remaining items throughout the year as a way of deepening your understanding.

1. Consider the three aspects of the spiritual life: prayer, service, and asceticism. Which one of these three "legs" of your spiritual life is most in need of attention? Describe an action you can take to strengthen this part of your spirituality.

   Pretty well same
   Need more prayer for
   others

2. The spiritual life is both a personal and a communal response to God. Complete the following statements.

   ❖ The faith community strengthens me by

   Encouragement —

   ❖ I strengthen the faith community by

   backing them + being there to share
   Being there to help when asked
   or when there is a need

3. In the video, Governor Gilligan shared several "pages" from his own spiritual journal. If you were to think of your own life of faith as a journal, how would some of its chapters be titled, and what story would they tell? Think of three examples and describe them in this space.

❖ *Prayer in family*
prayer holding family together

❖ *Prayer in time of crisis or difficulties*
Knowing God is there to help, I'm not alone.

❖ *Prayers with other believers*
Strengthens my faith & prayer time

4. Interview someone you believe is a person of prayer. What questions would you ask?

A maturing Christian is one whose responses to the challenges and invitations of life effect the kind of loving and working that Jesus and his Church have modeled.

EVELYN AND JAMES WHITEHEAD

The article on the next page explores the theme of thankfulness in the Christian life.

▶ ▶ ▶ ▶ ▶ ▶

A THANKFUL HEART

by Rev. Robert J. Hater

A thankful heart lies at the center of the Christian life. I was fortunate to learn this lesson when I was only five years old— on Thanksgiving Day.

All day long, we looked forward to the wonderful Thanksgiving meal that Mom was preparing. Shortly before we were to sit down at table, the front doorbell rang. My four-year-old sister, Mary Ann, and I ran to answer it. A boy about eleven and a girl about ten stood there. The girl held a baby, covered with a shawl. The boy said, "We are poor and have no money for food this Thanksgiving. Will you give us money so we can buy food?"

Mary Ann and I called our mother. Mom answered, "We don't have much money, but we would like you to share what we have. We invite you to join us for our Thanksgiving." The children seemed surprised, and the boy said they could not stay. Mom replied, "Then let us prepare meals for you to take along with you."

While the children waited in the hall, Mom, Mary Ann, and I went into the kitchen and packed the meals. I felt good as we gathered turkey, dressing, cranberries, potatoes, beans, a piece of cake, and soda pop. Mom prepared a bottle of milk for the baby. Mary Ann and I were joyful when we gave the food to the children. They took it and left.

Since it was a beautiful day, my sister and I went onto the front porch to watch the children leave. They went down the steps and walked up the street toward the intersection. When they arrived there, the girl suddenly threw the baby to the boy.

We screamed, "They're hurting the baby, they're hurting the baby!" Hurrying inside, we told Mom and Dad.

All of us returned immediately to the porch. As we got there, the girl, now holding the baby, tucked it under her arm. As she did, the boy, who carried the food, laughed in the strangest way. Then he took the Thanksgiving meals we had so lovingly prepared and

> *The important thing is to give with a thankful heart.*

Reverend Robert J. Hater is a Cincinnati diocesan priest and a professor of religious studies at the University of Dayton, Ohio. He is an internationally known lecturer and writer. He was the religious education director for the Archdiocese of Cincinnati from 1973 to 1979 and initiated the Lay Pastoral Ministry Program for the Archdiocese. He received the 1994 Catechetical Award from the National Conference of Catechetical Leadership. Father Hater holds a Doctorate in Philosophy from St. John's University, Jamaica, New York.

threw them down the sewer. They continued laughing as they disappeared around the corner.

My sister and I cried, "They hurt the baby and threw away our food!" As we cried, Mom and Dad embraced us. Mom said, "Bob and Mary Ann, it's okay. We are going to have a wonderful Thanksgiving." We continued to cry, "But they hurt the baby and threw away our food!"

Mom said, "The children tricked us. That wasn't a baby; it was a doll. They didn't want food; they wanted money. Nevertheless, you are going to learn a very important lesson today." When we quieted down, Mom spoke words that made an indelible impression on us. She said, "We gave the children a wonderful gift today, sharing a big part of our Thanksgiving meal with them. This was a wonderful gift, even though they did not accept it. The important thing is that we gave with a thankful heart."

Mom continued, "God did that long ago, when he gave us the greatest gift—his own Son. Just as the children rejected our gift today some people rejected Jesus too. Some continue to reject him today by lying, cheating, or hurting one another. But God keeps on giving, and Jesus is the greatest gift we could receive. Let's remember God's gift and all our gifts today as we go in and have a wonderful Thanksgiving meal together."

This attitude of thankfulness is our fundamental perspective as Christians. It is our first prayer, the acknowledgment of our total dependency on God, and our acceptance of the great love which God desires to share with us.

Give thanks in all circumstances; for this is the will of God in Christ Jesus for you.

1 THESSALONIANS 5:18

FOR REFLECTION

What great gifts is God offering you in your life? How do you express your thanks for these gifts?

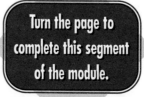

Turn the page to
complete this segment
of the module.

But truly
God has listened;
he has given heed to
the words of my prayer.

Blessed be God,
because he has not rejected
my prayer
or removed his
steadfast love from me.

PSALM 66:19–20

LISTENING AND RESPONDING

Prayer always flows from our experience. If we express what we are truly feeling, our prayer might be one of praise or one of lament. Which is your prayer today? Write it here.

PRAYING WITH OTHERS

Choose a symbolic object that expresses the prayer you wrote in the box above. The next time you gather with your group, bring the objects each of you have chosen and place them on your prayer table. Offer your prayers together.

Moving On

THIS SEGMENT REFLECTED ON THE QUALITIES OF A PRAYERFUL LIFE. THE NEXT SEGMENT INTRODUCES THE OUR FATHER AS THE CENTRAL PRAYER OF THE CHRISTIAN TRADITION.

THE OUR FATHER

Coming into the presence of the Hallowed One is an awesome and wondrous thing. In prayer we approach God, gathering up all that we are and acknowledging in humility who God is. Such is the gift of praying the Our Father.

The seven petitions of the Our Father reveal the heart of the Gospel (see *CCC*, 2761). We begin by blessing the name of God. We pray for the truth, charity, freedom, and justice that mark the coming of God's kingdom. We pray that God's will be done, and that the gift of God's nourishment will empower us physically and spiritually to continue God's work. We pray to be forgiven as we too forgive, and to be freed from all the temptations that separate us from God. We conclude by asking for deliverance from evil, especially that of selfishness.

The Our Father beckons us into the mystery of God. It calls us to believe in the now, to experience God with us, and to reach out in hope for the final coming of the reign of God through Christ's return.

LEARNING OBJECTIVES
After completing this segment of the module, you will be able to:

1. Explain why the Our Father is the central Christian prayer

2. Describe the seven petitions of the Our Father

3. Reflect on the ways the Our Father expresses your own relationship with God

YOUR THOUGHTS
Spend a few moments thinking about the following.

How and when did you learn to pray the Our Father? How do you include it in your life of prayer?

The Lord's Prayer is the most perfect of prayers . . . In it we ask, not only for all the things we can rightly desire, but also in the sequence that they should be desired.

SAINT THOMAS AQUINAS
SUMMA THEOLOGIAE

LOOKING AHEAD

LOOKING AHEAD

*Run through
all the holy prayers
[in Scripture],
and I do not think
that you will find
anything in them
that is not contained
and included
in the Lord's Prayer.*

SAINT AUGUSTINE

This video segment is a reflection on the seven petitions of the Our Father. You will find an outline of this video content below. You may wish to refer to this outline as you view the video. Use the space provided to jot down any questions or thoughts that occur to you during your viewing. When you have finished, record your initial reactions to the video before moving on to the questions on pages 28 and 29.

VIDEO OUTLINE

Introduction

The Our Father is the foundation of all Christian prayer.

The seven petitions of the Our Father are a summary of the whole Gospel.

The Our Father is an important part of the worship of the Christian community.

The Our Father expresses the attitudes we bring to our celebration of the Eucharist.

The Seven Petitions of the Our Father

1. **Thy kingdom come ...**
   All prayer should begin with an acknowledgment of God's goodness and mercy. — *1st epiume e Gods goodness*

2. **Thy kingdom come ...**
   Jesus, who ushered in the kingdom of God, widened the boundaries of the kingdom to include the marginalized.

3. **Thy will be done on earth, as it is in heaven.**
   We open our will to seek and do the will of God.

4. **Give us this day our daily bread ...**
   We acknowledge that all we have comes as a gift from God.

5. **Forgive us our trespasses as we forgive those who trespass against us ...**
   We affirm that we cannot receive forgiveness if we cannot offer it to others.

6. **Lead us not into temptation ...**
   We ask God's help for those times when we will be tempted and faith will be difficult.

7. **Deliver us from evil.**
   We join with the whole Church in asking to be freed from all past, present, and future evil, and to be blessed with peace and perseverance.

THOUGHTS AND QUESTIONS DURING VIEWING

✎

May your name be known

Pray our own will

Jesus loves beyond all boundaries

Opening our will to presence of God
"Go to God" God does not own
our will. Must give our will
Actively not passively
Pray how you feel us open to
your will

Daily bread – Gift not something

FIRST IMPRESSIONS AFTER VIEWING

✎ I've earned or is entitled to.

Deliver us from moments when

faith is difficult

attitudes community wants
open to Kingdom not just
for ourselves.
Sign of peace - Sign of reconciliation

LOOKING BACK

Father, if you are willing,
remove this cup from me;
yet, not my will
but yours be done."

LUKE 22:42

Review the questions or comments that occurred to you as you viewed this part of the video segment. When time allows, discuss your thoughts with another person. Now respond to several of the questions or activities on these two pages. Return to the remaining items throughout the year as a way of deepening your understanding.

1. Describe a time when it was easy for you to follow God's will, and a time when it was difficult.

   Difficult when others have hurt me
   or when I'm challenged
   Easy when everything is going
   smoothly (when I'm surrounded by
   others of strong faith)

2. Justice is a central aspect of the reign of God. What do you feel called to do in your own life to bring justice
   ❖ into your home?

   Encourage others to grow in faith

   ❖ into your workplace?

   ❖ into your neighborhood?

3. Which is more difficult: to forgive someone or to ask someone for forgiveness? Explain your answer.

ask for forgiveness

4. The Our Father is a prayer of faith. What are some ways you are living the faith you profess by this prayer?

But strive first for the kingdom of God and his righteousness, and all these things will be given to you as well.

MATTHEW 6:33

5. Without using words, illustrate your understanding of one of the petitions of the Our Father.

The article on the next page offers a reflection on the seven petitions of the Our Father.

▶ ▶ ▶ ▶ ▶ ▶

Reflections on the Our Father

by Bishop Robert F. Morneau

Simple and faithful trust, humble and joyous assurance are the proper dispositions for one who prays the Our Father.

CCC, 2797

Saint Paul urges us to "pray unceasingly." We can do no better in following his advice than by praying from the heart the fundamental Christian prayer—the Our Father. When the disciples asked Jesus how to pray, he taught them—and now us—a prayer that contains seven elements, each holding a petition. Each is a map pointing the way on a part of our spiritual journey.

1. *Our Father, who art in heaven, hallowed be thy name.* God is the one who has given us life and, like a human father and mother, we owe our existence to God and to our parents. Jesus teaches us that God is *our* Father, which makes us all sisters and brothers with one another. Our creator God dwells in heaven but is also here on earth among us in Jesus and the gift of the Holy Spirit. Recognizing God's name as Father, as a Brother in Jesus, as a Friend in the Holy Spirit, we honor, or hallow, God's many names: Father, Son, Spirit, Creator, Redeemer, Sanctifier, Water, Fire, Wind.

Jesus, teach us to know your Father and your Spirit. Give us the gift of reverence to speak your name with love and respect. Help us to long for heaven and the gift of eternity as well as to treasure our lives here on earth. Jesus, teach us how to pray.

Add your own reflections here.

2. Thy kingdom come. Saint Paul reminds us that the kingdom of God is not one of eating and drinking. Rather, it is a kingdom of peace, love, and joy (Romans 14:17). God's kingdom comes when God rules and guides our hearts and our history. Too often we can choose to stand under the banner of another kingdom: the kingdom of greed, violence, pride, sloth. God's kingdom is one of peace, and it involves four qualities: truth, charity, freedom, and justice.

Jesus, empower us through your Spirit to be kingdom people. May we speak the truth and not live in the land of falsity and illusion; may we be a loving and caring community and not yield to apathy and indifference; may we gain freedom from our addictions and sin by means of discipline and grace; and may we do the works of justice by respecting and promoting the rights of all. Jesus, teach us how to pray.

Add your own reflections here.

---

3. Thy will be done on earth, as it is in heaven. The prophet Micah tells us basically what God wants from us: that we act with justice, that we love with tenderness, that we walk humbly in faith with our God (Micah 6:8). That's all! One of the great struggles on our Christian journey is that tension between doing our own will ("I did it *my* way!") or doing God's will. When the front wheels on our car are not aligned, the car begins to shake, rattle, and roll. When our wheels are aligned—when God's wheel and our wheel are going in the same direction—both cars and souls experience peace.

Jesus, guide us in your way—the way of justice, compassion, and forgiveness. Help us to know God's will in the daily events of our lives. May your Spirit enlighten us to see what you ask of us, and may that same Spirit give us the courage and strength to do your will. Jesus, teach us how to pray.

Add your own reflections here.

The holiness of God is the inaccessible center of his eternal mystery.

CCC, 2809

4. *Give us this day our daily bread.* We hunger for life at every level: physical, psychological, and spiritual. We need our daily cereal and milk, we need to belong and experience love, we need union with God. Our God not only creates but also sustains us. We acknowledge in this petition God's providential caring. God will give us what we need: food, love, belonging, wisdom, peace.

Jesus, we know our poverty and dependence upon you and your Father. Satisfy our longings of body and soul with your grace, especially with the gift of the bread of life, the Eucharist. May we always be grateful for all you give us. Jesus, teach us how to pray.

Add your own reflections here.

5. *. . . and forgive us our trespasses, as we forgive those who trespass against us.* The Our Father is a dangerous prayer. We ask God to forgive us just as we forgive others. We all sin and stand in need of God's mercy. If we refuse to forgive those who hurt us, something happens in our hearts that prevents us from experiencing God's abundant mercy.

Jesus, through your death on the cross you conquered sin and death. As you forgave those who injured you, help us to forgive one another. Only the strength of your Spirit and the gift of your compassion can enable us to be a forgiving community. Jesus, teach us how to pray.

Add your own reflections here.

6. . . . and lead us not into temptation . . . As we journey as a pilgrim people back toward God there are temptations along the way that entice us away from God. We fail to put first things first or, worse, we choose some idol instead of the living and true God. God has given us certain *means* that can help us get to heaven: pleasure, power, possessions, prestige, people. But if these *means* become *ends*, we have yielded to temptation and endanger our salvation.

Jesus, may we never become confused in making your gifts more important than you, the Giver. When temptations come our way, give us the strength to turn always to you. If we fail, may we rise quickly in your mercy and resolve to be your faithful servants. Jesus, teach us how to pray.

Add your own reflections here.

---

7. . . . but deliver us from evil. Jesus came to set us free, to win us deliverance from evil, darkness, and death. Every day we confront good and evil; every day we need the gifts of the Spirit to be delivered from sin. None of us is immune from doing great evil. Only through constant prayer, fasting, and generosity can we stay on the path Jesus has marked out for us.

Jesus, you are our redeemer and savior. Draw us close to you so that we might put on your mind and heart and thereby be delivered from evil. Free us all, body and soul, from sin's alienating darkness. Jesus, teach us how to pray.

Add your own reflections here.

Be kind to one another, tenderhearted, forgiving one another, as God in Christ has forgiven you.

EPHESIANS 4:32

Turn the page to complete this segment of the module.

▶ ▶ ▶ ▶ ▶ ▶

LOOKING BEYOND

> *Let us sing a new song not with our lips but with our lives.*
>
> SAINT AUGUSTINE

LISTENING AND RESPONDING

Becoming a person of prayer is a continuing process. As you complete this module, what are the next steps you would like to take to deepen your prayer life?

PRAYING WITH OTHERS

Assign various members of your group one of the seven petitions of the Our Father, and invite them each to write a prayer reflection on that petition as you did in the previous pages. Share these prayers together as an extended meditation on this central Christian prayer.

Moving On

THIS SEGMENT REFLECTED ON THE OUR FATHER AS THE CENTRAL PRAYER OF THE CHRISTIAN TRADITION. THE CLOSING REFLECTION SUGGESTS THE ANGELUS AS A WAY OF MARKING THE BEGINNING AND END OF EACH DAY IN THE LIFE OF FAITH.

Closing Reflection

THE ANGELUS

Praying the Angelus is a way of participating in an honored prayer tradition of the Church. The Angelus reminds us of Mary's willingness to conform her will to that of God. Make this prayer your own and pray it with others to be reminded of God's constant call in your life.

READER: The angel spoke God's message to Mary,
ALL: and she conceived of the Holy Spirit.

ALL: Hail, Mary . . .

READER: "I am the lowly servant of the Lord:
ALL: let it be done to me according to your word."

ALL: Hail, Mary . . .

READER: And the Word became flesh
ALL: and lived among us.

ALL: Hail, Mary . . .

READER: Pray for us, holy Mother of God,
ALL: that we may become worthy of the promises of Christ.

READER: Let us pray,

Lord,
fill our hearts with your grace:
once, through the message of an angel
you revealed to us the incarnation of your Son;
now, through his suffering and death
lead us to the glory of his resurrection.

We ask this through Christ our Lord.
ALL: Amen.

PRAYER NOTES

For where
your treasure is,
there will your heart
be also.

MATTHEW 6:21

You may wish to use these two pages to begin the practice of a prayer journal. Or you may use them to record additional reflections as you complete this module.

Prayer Notes

This is the day that
the Lord has made;
let us rejoice
and be glad in it.

PSALM 118: 24

RESOURCE BIBLIOGRAPHY

Church Documents

Abbot, Walter M., S.J., gen. ed. *The Documents of Vatican II*. New York: Herder and Herder, 1966.

Congregation for the Clergy. *General Directory for Catechesis*. Washington, D.C.: USCC, 1997.

Pope John Paul II. *On Catechesis in Our Time (Catechesi Tradendae)*. Washington, D.C.: USCC, 1979.

Libreria Editrice Vaticana. *Catechism of the Catholic Church*. Allen, Texas: Thomas More, 1994.

National Conference of Catholic Bishops. *Sharing the Light of Faith: National Catechetical Directory for Catholics of the United States*. Washington, D.C.: USCC, 1979.

Theological Resources

Barry, William A., S.J. *God's Passionate Desire: And Our Response*. Notre Dame, Ind.: Ave Maria, Press, 1993.

—*Who Do You Say I Am?* Notre Dame, Ind.: Ave Maria Press, 1996.

Cistercian Studies: No. 59. *Sayings of the Desert Fathers*. Kalamazoo, Minn.: Cistercian Publications.

Huebsch, Bill. *Vatican II in Plain English*. Three volumes. Allen, Tex.: Thomas More, 1997.

Keating, Thomas. *The Heart of the World: A Spiritual Catechism*. New York: Crossroad Publishing, 1984.

Leech, Kenneth. *Experiencing God: Theology as Spirituality*. New York: Harper & Row, 1985.

McBride, Alfred, O.P. *Essentials of the Faith: A Guide to the Catechism of the Catholic Church*. Huntington, Ind.: Our Sunday Visitor, Inc., 1994.

Merton, Thomas. *Life and Holiness*. Garden City, N.Y.: Doubleday, 1962.

—*Thoughts in Solitude*. New York: Noonday Press, 1956.

—*What Is Contemplation?* Springfield, Ill.: Templegate Publishers, 1978.

Mourneau, Robert F. *Ashes to Easter: Lenten Meditations*. New York: Crossroad Publishing, 1996.

—*A Retreat with Jessica Powers: Loving a Passionate God*. Cincinnati: St. Anthony Messenger Press, 1995.

Nhat Hanh, Thich. *The Long Road Turns to Joy: A Guide to Walking Meditation*. Copyright 1996 by Thick Nhat Hanh.

Norris, Kathleen. *The Cloister Walk*. New York: Riverhead Books, 1996.

Nouwen, Henri J.M. *Gracias! A Latin American Journal*. San Francisco: Harper & Row, 1983.

—*The Inner Voice of Love: A Journey Through Anguish to Freedom*. New York: Doubleday,

Whitehead, Evelyn Eaton and James D. Whitehead. *Christian Life Patterns*. New York: Crossroad Publishing, 1992.

Wicks, Robert. *Touching the Holy*. Notre Dame, Ind.: Ave Maria Press, 1992.

Videos

The Mystery of Faith: An Introduction to Catholicism. A ten-part video series featuring Father Michael Himes. Fisher Productions, Box 727, Jefferson Valley, New York 10535.

The Faithful Revolution: Vatican II. Allen, Texas: RCL Enterprises, Vatican II Productions, 1997.

Computer Resources

Catechism of the Catholic Church for Personal Computers. United States Catholic Conference, 1994. Available on disk and CD/ROM in English, Spanish, French.

Destination Vatican II. CD/ROM. Allen, Tex.: RCL • Resources for Christian Living, 1997.

ASSESSMENT TOOL

This tool is provided as an aid for you, the catechist, to review the insights, questions, and concerns you may have after completing the entire video-print module. It may be useful as a reference in a discussion with your program director and as a record of completing this learning module. Photocopy this page for your personal records and for your program director's records before mailing to the *Echoes of Faith* project.

Name_____

Level Taught _____

Home Phone _____

Parish_____

City _____

Religious Education Program Director _____

1. What are the three most important insights or suggestions that you carry away with you as you complete this learning module *Prayer and Spirituality?*

2. List up to five issues or questions that you would still like to discuss with your program director.

3. In a sentence or two describe how this learning module will be helpful to you in your service as a catechist.

We would appreciate your insights and suggestions. This page is a postage-paid mailer. Please detach it from the booklet and mail the completed page to the *Echoes of Faith* project.

I have completed the learning module *Prayer and Spirituality.*

Date Begun   _____

Date Completed _____

Catechist

_____
(signature)

Program Director

_____
(signature)

BUSINESS REPLY MAIL

FIRST-CLASS MAIL   PERMIT NO 100   ALLEN TX

POSTAGE WILL BE PAID BY ADDRESSEE

ATTN PUBLISHER

ECHOES OF FAITH™ PROJECT

RCL • RESOURCES FOR CHRISTIAN LIVING™

PO BOX 7000

ALLEN TX 75013-9811

Fold